Opium

As an actor Andrew has appeare
(with the exception of Pitlochry), The Royal National Theatre
and The Royal Court. He has also appeared with The Royal
Shakespeare Company. He has directed some sixty productions
in Repertory Theatres including Liverpool Playhouse, Leeds
Playhouse and the Dundee Repetory. His production of
Ionesco's *The Chairs* was recently seen in Holland and New
York. He has written sixty-five plays, won three Fringe Firsts and
a B.A.F.T.A. (Scotland) for the radio version of *Opium Eater*
starring Neil Cunningham and Russell Hunter. His most
performed play titles include *Hello Dali*, *Boys in the Backroom*
and *Metaphysics & Strip*. His most recent work, the
controversial *Wanted Dead or Alive* about Osama Bin Laden has
so far been performed in Edinburgh, Arundel, London and
Glasgow. He lives in Edinburgh.

Capercaillie Books

Opium Eater

by Andrew Dallmeyer

Capercaillie Books

CAPERCAILLIE BOOKS LIMITED

First published by Capercaillie Books Limited in 2005.

Registered Office 1 Rutland Court, Edinburgh.

© 2005 Andrew Dallmeyer. The moral right of the author has been asserted.

Design by Ian Kirkwood Design.

Typeset by Chimera Creations in Cosmos and Veljovic.

Printed in Great Britain by Antony Rowe Ltd., Chippenham, Wiltshire.

A catalogue record for this book is available from the British Library.

ISBN 0-9549625-3-2

The publisher acknowledges support from the Scottish Arts Council towards the publication of this title.

Scottish
Arts Council

Dedicated to the memory of the late Neil Cunningham, the original De Quincey.

Introduction

When Peter Lichtenfels, the then director of the Traverse in Edinburgh, suggested to me that Thomas De Quincey might make an interesting subject for a play, I had no idea that he had anything to do with Edinburgh, far less that he was buried in the cemetery at the bottom of Lothian Road. His grave is not far from the little turret, built to provide a lookout for grave robbers, and somebody, to this day, puts white poppies on De Quincey's grave from time to time. I have thought of trying to find out who this is, but you might have to wait for a while!

I started to read De Quincey's writing and his voice emerged very strongly to me. With his erudition, his classical learning, his philosophical knowledge, his conversation would have been 'mind blowing'. In fact to have heard Coleridge, his contemporary, and De Quincey in conversation would have been an awesome experience. I felt I could successfully emulate his elaborate and baroque style where every noun has an adjective, and sometimes two! Nothing is ever expressed simply, when it can be embellished. I've only used the occasional quotation.

Unfortunately, as is often the case with such people who live so much in the mind, he was hopeless when it came to the practical realities of life. Much of his time was spent in cheap digs and even the Poorhouse, although he later married and settled in Lasswade. He was a kind of nineteenth century 'hippy' and heavily dependant on his beloved laudanum, in those days available at every chemist shop despite being an addictive mixture of opium and alcohol. It was drunk and not eaten, so in a way 'Opium Eater' is a misnomer. A bit of an outsider then, struggling with deadlines and empty pages. I could identify with that, although I've never experimented with opium myself!

When I read *Confessions of an English Opium-Eater*, there was, to be frank, little of interest in it, until I got to his descriptions of his opium dreams, 'the sceneries' as Willy calls them. Here, I realised was great theatrical potential. And the ability of the imagination to carry us anywhere while we are confined in one place, is one of my favourite themes. In fact if I had to say one thing that my plays are about, it is the power of the imagination. Moreover, De Quincey realised that his fantasies came from what was later to be named by Freud as the subconscious mind. In this respect, he is the forerunner of Freud.

But, as is so often the case for the playwright, the scope of the play was determined by financial restraints. I was told I could have 'two actors and no scenery'. I toyed with the idea of De Quincey in the room with a young woman. There is a lengthy description of such a relationship in one of his books. His interest in the poor creature was purely platonic and altruistic. But in the end I created Willy, who was a combination of several people I had met.

While assembling my Community show *Blockbuster* at Theatre Workshop, Edinburgh, an extraordinary character turned up and volunteered to act in the play. He was unemployed and receiving medication up at the Royal Infirmary. We spent a great deal of time together and I was often struck by the innocuousness of our relationship. Not only that, but I often had the distinct impression that I was being gently 'sent up' by this character, who most people would call a simpleton.

One more ingredient is worth mentioning. The play was first performed in the tiny Traverse Downstairs Theatre. Everybody who worked in there complained of the noise from above. There was a bar upstairs. Rather than trying to ignore the noise, I decided to incorporate it and upstairs became a brothel. So now, wherever the play is performed noises from above are required, obviously through a speaker.

These then are the ingredients that went into the mix – the way the play was created. Two outcasts, bound together by poverty and trying to overcome their mutual language barrier. The wise fool and the foolish wise man. Their relationship has been compared to the relationship in *Of Mice and Men* and between Prospero and Caliban in *The Tempest*. Whatever the case, with each drawing inspiration from the other, it is by turns funny, touching, sad and moving. And, of course, Willy is the winner, ending up, as he does, with the bed, the room, the spoon, the lace and the gold watch. Not bad for a 'daft laddie'!

In the end it is my belief that a successful play must use much of its author's passion and compassion. *Opium Eater* is not a dry biographical academic exercise, but an emotional experience where the pleasures and pains of drug addiction are accurately explored, and two men in a room can conjure up a universe. And from their drab and dismal surroundings can flower the exotic blooms of their dream-laden imaginations. Something from nothing.

Andrew Dallmeyer, 2005

Note on first production

Opium Eater was first performed at the Traverse Theatre, Edinburgh in June 1984 with the following cast:

De Quincey, man of letters: Neil Cunningham

Willy, man of the streets: Stewart Preston

Characters

DE QUINCEY: the author of *Confessions of an English Opium-Eater*.

WILLY: his temporary man servant.

Act 1

Scene 1

December 1820. A rented room in the Grassmarket, Edinburgh. Simple furniture: chair, table and bed. An impression of dirt, dust and chaos. Piles of papers and books. Items of clothing. DE QUINCEY sits at the table writing feverishly. Suddenly he stops, listens intently, resumes writing and stops again.

DE QUINCEY: Hark! What noise is that?

(He listens for a moment or two, then continues to work. He stops again.)

There! Once more. A scratching and a scraping. Or do my ears deceive me?

(He continues to work. Stops again.)

Yet again. No doubt of it. I fear it is a rat. Cunning little devil! See how he is motionless and silent whenever I am listening out for him.

(He resumes his work.)

And yet he seems to move from one place to another. From left to right across the room. There he goes again!

(He stops.)

And always stopping when I stop.

(Suddenly the penny drops.)

What! Have I taken leave of my senses? What a mighty perturbation is there in my brain! 'Tis but the scraping of the quill upon the paper! Ah me! What a pitiful thing is the damnable life of the hack! For a few meagre pounds I must wring from my very soul paragraph upon paragraph of fresh-filigreed coinage, and from the grim reality of these drab and dismal surrounds I must cultivate the exotic blooms of my dream-laden imagination. And all for what? An indifferent public, hostile critics, and ten pounds from Mister Blackwood. And that alone is what spurs me onward.

Now, where was I? Ah, yes. Struggling with this accursed sentence. The drudgery of committing the words to paper is almost unbearable to me for my mind is capable of much swifter motion than my hand and by the time my hand has caught up with my brains my brain has long since departed into another realm.

(Speaking as he writes.)

'He would lay down his life if he might get up and walk but he is as . . .

(He pauses.)

as timid as a kitten.'

(He crosses it out.)

No! That will not suffice. Kittens are more often playful than timid. Besides it is a cliché. 'He is as timid as a mouse'. Just as bad. Most of the mice I meet are as bold as brass. The Scotch ones at any rate. 'He is as timid as a tortoise'. No, no. Still worse. Alliteration for alliteration's sake. Such tendencies should be eradicated immediately. 'He is as timid as . . . as timid as . . .'

(Banging and crashing from above.)

Damnation!

(He looks up at the ceiling.)

There it goes again! This perpetual thumping and banging. Crash! Thump! Wallop! Like a herd of stampeding elephants.

How may a man be expected to work with such endless distraction constantly afoot? 'He is as timid as . . .' Possibly timid is the word at fault. Try feeble. Or frail. Or 'fragile as a bubble'. No! Too fanciful for Mr. Blackwood's taste I fear. 'He is as fragile as a . . .' I am totally devoid of all inspiration. There is no alternative left to me but to chance my arm in a game of hazard. Where is 'old Oxford'

(He looks through a pile of books on his desk)

Ah! My trusty friend. Pray give me a word. 'He is as fragile as . . .

(He flicks through the dictionary, placing his finger at random.)

Onslaught! He is as fragile as an onslaught? Scarcely suitable. Try once again.

'He is as fragile as a . . .

(He flicks through the dictionary again)

Orange! 'He is as fragile as an orange?' No luck today. Where is this word?

(More banging upstairs.)

This infernal commotion from on high will surely drive me to the very brink of madness. Bedlam itself could surely not provide a more discordant cacophony and yet I am powerless to prevent it. Powerless! The very word!

(Writing)

'For he is as powerless as . . . an infant' – good – 'and cannot even attempt to rise?' Excellent! The paragraph is now complete and another milestone is passed on the tortuous road to journey's end. Now the essay lacks but an ending, A final flourish. It must end with a flourish. This calls for a fresh sheet of paper. There.

(Pause)

Nowhere is a man more directly faced with his own inadequacies than when he is confronted with an empty page, for the state of the paper and the state of his mind are exactly analogous.

(Pause)

Perhaps I have already concocted a suitable ending in a previous work? What a blessing that would be. I could cobble it on. But I fear it is too much to hope for. Now to attempt the fully perpendicular. Ah! My poor legs! Tis the rheumatism that grips me.

(He rises slowly and moves towards a pile of papers.)

Many of my finest works I have left behind me in lieu of rent. A futile attempt to placate a succession of irate Edinburgh landladies. My erratic progress forms a veritable paper chase across this fair city which even the most diligent sleuth would be hard pressed to unravel. From sordid basement to squalid attic the thoughts of De Quincey lie scattered like so much superfluous confetti. And what has become of these riches? Fuel for the fire no doubt.

(In pain with his legs.)

Ah me! If suffering be good for the soul, then my soul must surely be saved!

What is this? 'Logic of Political Economy' already rejected by Blackwood. But would he remember it I wonder? I fear he would. What is here? 'National Temperance Movements' – hardly relevant to the matter in hand. What is here? A shoe horn! How come I by this? 'Kant's Idea of a Universal History on a Cosmopolitical Plane'. Too esoteric to be of much interest to a general readership I fear. A stuffed bird! A paper on murder and two unfinished articles on Milton. There is nothing here. Nothing of consequence. Perhaps I should let the matter rest for a while. Defer the finale until after a respite. But could I enjoy leisure under such circumstances? I fear I could not for my tormented mind would forever remind me of the duty I should be engaged in.

(Banging upstairs)

Once more the shouting in the close. The laughter on the stairs and the clatter on the ceiling. Will it never cease? Perhaps there might exist a suitable ending already written by another? Perish the thought. Perish the thought.

It is worthy of serious consideration.

It would surely facilitate matters considerably.

You are not suggesting . . . plagiarism. It is unworthy of you.

Everybody else does it.

That is no excuse.

Indeed Mister Coleridge has seldom done otherwise.

Yes. But I am not Mister Coleridge.

Think of all the work that you would save yourself. Hour upon hour of grinding monotony. Would it not be a pleasant relief to have the thing finished for once and for all?

Get thee behind me Satan!

Go on! Have a look. Have a look in your books.

I must not.

Go on!

I will not.

Go on! Where is the harm in it?

Well . . . just this once.

(He looks through his books.)

'Complete works of Shakespeare'.

Too well known to risk. The deception would be noted.

'Holy Bible'.

I will not blaspheme.

Sir Isaac Newton's 'Theory of Gravity'.

Too ponderous a tome.

(He drops it on the floor.)

What have we here? A dead beetle in a saucer.

'An Anthology of German Writing', Ah! That could be the very thing! Something sufficiently obscure to be unfamiliar to English readers. A piece from the much overpraised work of Goethe. Now let me see. It will need translation of course. There would be much work involved. Besides I should only feel guilty in claiming the piece as my own. I cannot do it. It is not in my nature. I must fall back onto my own resources which I fear are sadly diminished.

(More banging)
This wretche'd turmoil has the better of me. I cannot work under these conditions.

WILLY bursts into the room. a disconcerting presence, shabbily dressed. Most people would refer to him as a simpleton.

DE QUINCEY: Ah! Winged Mercury!

WILLY: **(breathless)** Aw the way frae Aberdeen. I've run aw the way frae Aberdeen.

DE QUINCEY: Come, come now Willy. You surely exaggerate.

WILLY: I'm no exaggerin'.

DE QUINCEY: A journey of such inordinate length was scarcely warranted

WILLY: 'Strue I'm tellin' ya. 'Strue.

DE QUINCEY: Then I must surely believe you.

WILLY: I came back here as fast as I could, I've minded the messages and aw Mister . . . eh . . . **(WILLY cannot remember DE QUINCEY'S NAME. He gropes for it.)** . . . eh . . .

DE QUINCEY: You have a message for me?

WILLY: Aye. The messages.

DE QUINCEY: Did you purchase the requisite provisions?

WILLY: Eh?

DE QUINCEY: Did you get all the things that I asked for?

WILLY: Aye. There was twa things. The breid.

DE QUINCEY: Aye. The breid.

WILLY: Aye. And somethin' else tae. Eh? In a bottle, eh? Somethin' else tae.

DE QUINCEY: The tincture!

WILLY: Aye. Right enough, Which pocket's the breid in? This yin or this yin? Eh? Which pocket?

The answer to this question is obvious as both the bottle and the bread are protruding from the pockets of WILLY'S overcoat.

DE QUINCEY: **(deliberately guessing wrong)** That one!

WILLY: You're wrong there. I foolt ya. See. Here it's.

He pulls the bread triumphantly from his pocket with a gleeful laugh.

DE QUINCEY: Willy! You are incorrigible!

WILLY hands the bread to DE QUINCEY. DE QUINCEY examines the loaf.

DE QUINCEY: Well done. Well done indeed. No little mouse has nibbled at the bread.

WILLY: Wisne easy I'm tellin' ye. I'm fair stervin' wi' hunger.

DE QUINCEY: Then you have exercised a considerable degree of self-control and you shall have your just reward in due course.

WILLY: I went up and doon the High Street a hundred and fifty times.

DE QUINCEY: Then you must surely be exhausted.

WILLY: I smelt they jammie taerts fresh frae Ma Spittal's oven and ma mooth was fair slaverin' like a dug. She gies us a pastry frae time tae time but she didne hae ony pastries the day.

DE QUINCEY: And the tincture? Where is the tincture?

WILLY: You'll be needin' that right enough. Which pocket? Which pocket?

DE QUINCEY: **(again pointing to the wrong one)** That one!

WILLY: Wrong again. Here it's!

He produces the bottle in triumph. DE QUINCEY reaches for the bottle WILLY withdraws it.

DE QUINCEY: Come along Willy. Do not be so childish.

DE QUINCEY reaches for the bottle. WILLY withdraws it.

DE QUINCEY: Come, come. Do not torment me so.

WILLY gives the bottle to DE QUINCEY. They both grip it for a second or two, WILLY being aware of DE QUINCEY'S addiction.

WILLY: Can I hae ma reward noo?

DE QUINCEY: Patience is a virtue
   Virtue is a grace
   And when all put together
   Make a very pretty face.
   Your imperial throne awaits you your highness.
   Pray be seated.
   (He indicates the chair.)
   Now, what has become of the knife?

WILLY: I could break it wi' ma hands.

DE QUINCEY: No, no! I would not hear of such a thing for we must try to preserve some small appearance of decorum even though our present predicament is hardly conducive to such social niceties. Now then, let me see.
   (He searches for a knife.)
   From which druggist did you make the purchase?

WILLY: Eh?

DE QUINCEY: Where did you get the bottle from?

WILLY: I canna mind.

DE QUINCEY: Was it Buchan or Gilchrist?

WILLY: The auld wifey wi' the beard.

DE QUINCEY: Ah! Mrs. Gilchrist. Then it is the East India. Good, I am glad. For I prefer it to the Turkish.

WILLY: She's got mair dugs in her heid than Edinburgh Castle.

DE QUINCEY: Who has?

WILLY: Ma Gilchrist.

DE QUINCEY: Undoubtedly, undoubtedly.

WILLY: Is your story feenished yet Mister . . . eh . . . ?

DE QUINCEY: It lacks but an ending.

WILLY: I could feenish it fur ya. I could make they wee curlies.

DE QUINCEY: Thank you for the offer but I must finish it myself.

WILLY: I've written a wee story. I've bin to the scull. I've done readin' and writin' and aw things like that.

DE QUINCEY: I am sure you have Willy. What day is it today? Is it Wednesday or Thursday?

WILLY: It's Tuesday, Tuesday.

DE QUINCEY: Tuesday? Impossible.

WILLY: "Strue I'm tellin' ya. "Strue.

DE QUINCEY: But it was Tuesday only recently. I would always know a Tuesday.

WILLY: It's Tuesday the day.

DE QUINCEY: I sincerely hope you are right. For if it be Tuesday then I have an extra day in hand. For Friday is the last day my essay may be delivered.

WILLY: Friday's past long since. Our Lord was crucified on Friday.

DE QUINCEY: Ah! Here is the knife.

He cuts the bread in half and gives half of it to WILLY. WILLY eats ravenously.

DE QUINCEY: Do not eat too fast! Your stomach will suffer. Now for my own satisfaction!

He removes the top of the tincture bottle and pours a few drops into a glass. He puts the top back on and holds up the glass to measure the dosage. He removes the top again and puts in a few more drops. He replaces the top and holds up the glass. He removes the top for the third time and puts in a last few drops. He replaces the top. These actions are accompanied by the following lines.

DE QUINCEY: A few drops of laudanum. Daily. As prescribed. Purely for medicinal purposes you understand. It does not harm. In fact quite the contrary. In small quantities it can be most beneficial. Indeed Doctor Wilson has insisted that I continue with my course of treatment. He considers it absolutely essential as far as my future well-being is concerned. Together we are making a concerted effort to curb the more excessive symptoms of neuralgia.

WILLY: Eh?

DE QUINCEY: Neuralgia. A nervous disorder. The word is derived from the Greek 'Neuro' meaning 'nerve' and 'algia' meaning 'sickness'. Neuralgia. A votre sante!

He drinks the tincture down in a gulp.

WILLY: You've got a face like the Grassmarket.

DE QUINCEY: Oh. Is that a compliment?

WILLY: 'Strue I'm tellin' ya. 'Strue.

DE QUINCEY: Then I am at a loss for words. Have you never seen a man taking medicine before?

WILLY: Aye. I've seen you afore.

DE QUINCEY: Then why are you looking at me in such an accusatory fashion?

WILLY: Can you see the sceneries Mister . . . eh . . . ?

DE QUINCEY: The 'sceneries'? What 'sceneries'?

WILLY: Aye. The sceneries you see when you tak the tincture?

DE QUINCEY: Ah! The dream scenery. Is that what you want?

WILLY: Aye. That's them.

DE QUINCEY: I thought as much. I am heartily glad that my laudanum visions are a source of such delight to you, but for my own part I can only say that they have a horrifying and disturbing aspect which leads me to avoid them at all costs for I cannot accurately predict the outcome of my imbibing too fast and too freely. However it is certainly not my intention that matters should degenerate to such an extent on this day, for there is much work yet to be done and I can ill afford to lose time.

WILLY: Whit work's that eh?

DE QUINCEY: Writing Willy. What else?

WILLY: Aw. That isne work.

DE QUINCEY: I can assure you that it is.

WILLY: That's a terrible shame. I love they sceneries.

DE QUINCEY: Then I am heartily sorry to disappoint you, but I cannot surely be expected to provide you with constant entertainment as well as all the other amenities you enjoy. I shall possibly have a few more drops. And then that will most definitely be that.

He pours a few more drops of laudanum.

WILLY: You'll be feenished that bottle afore long.

DE QUINCEY: Stuff and nonsense.

WILLY: So you will too.

DE QUINCEY: I have money to earn. Which reminds me Willy you have forgotten to give me my change.

WILLY: Eh?

DE QUINCEY: Change of a shilling. I gave you a shilling. I remember distinctly because it was all that was left to me in the world.

WILLY: **(changing the subject)** There's nae change. Nae change in the weather. It's rainin' cats and dugs in Currie. Cock-a-doodle-do!

DE QUINCEY: I beg your pardon?

WILLY: It's still dreich.

DE QUINCEY: 'Dreich'. What is 'dreich'?

WILLY: Dreich is . . . dreich.

DE QUINCEY: It is not a word that is known to me but it sounds unpleasant. Am I right?

WILLY: Aye.

DE QUINCEY: Is it cold?

WILLY: Aye. It's fair freezing.

DE QUINCEY: Good. I am glad. Then I should be happy out of doors. For there are few things in the world that are more exhilarating to me than the cutting embrace of a freezing day, for then all my senses are sharpened and honed and my intellect is at the keenest height of its powers. And I can think of nothing more intoxicating than stepping forward over a crisp silver carpet of frost along a secluded country lane, where the breath billows out in an icicle cloud like fire from a dragons nostrils. Give me the winter any day! It is a warm summer's day that I cannot abide for it is then that death is closest to hand. For in summer the exuberant and riotous prodigality of life, forces the mind upon the antagonistic notion of death. Death breaths through a warm wind. It lies with luscious vegetation and the infinity implicit in summers' high skies and vaulted clouds chills my bones to the very marrow.

WILLY: Could ye no wear a coat?

DE QUINCEY: I beg your pardon?

WILLY: Could ye no wear a coat?

DE QUINCEY: I fear this matter runs too deep for such superficial treatment. However, the suggestion is much appreciated.

WILLY: Fine, fine. It's aw fur free.

DE QUINCEY: Free Willy?

WILLY: Aye. Free.

DE QUINCEY: That reminds me of the change

WILLY: Change?

DE QUINCEY: Yes change. What of the change?

WILLY: (changing the subject) There's a bawbee o' it away doon tae Musselbra'. I ken a wimmin in Musselbra' wi' forty-three bairns. Forty-three bairns she's brought intae the world an' aw of thim lassies tae. Then her eldest started hayin bairns o' her ane afore her mither wis feenshed. There's twa hunerd and thirty-seven bairns in the hoose awragither. I wis there fur ma dinner on Thursday last week. They gi' us aw a plate o' stovies.

DE QUINCEY: Two hundred and thirty seven children?

WILLY: Aye.

DE QUINCEY: Such a story is hard to credit.

WILLY: 'Strue I'm tellin' ya. 'Strue.

DE QUINCEY: Then the commotion must be truly appalling. Does she per-chance live in a shoe?

WILLY: Aw, Yer just jokin' me Mister . . . eh . . .

DE QUINCEY: Imagine all the horrendous problems of being raised in such an enormous family.

WILLY: Aye. I was raised in a hen hoose masell. I had neither mither nor faither.

DE QUINCEY: Such a thing is not possible.

WILLY: 'Strue I'm tellin' ye. 'Strue. I wis takin' frae unner a gooseberry bush. I slep' in ben the hens. First thing in the mornin' 'Cock-a-doodle-do'. I git up and pick up they eggies. If I didne smash ony I got yin fur masel' . . . Then I had tae clean oot aw the dirt frae the flair. I had grain fur ma breakfast same as the hens. Once I was feedin' the muckle broon cockerels when they sterted chasin' us roon the Meenister's gairdin. They chased us roon' an' roon' aw in among the flooers. Then the Meenister's wife sees us oot o' the windae an' she comes rinnin' frae the hoose wi' a muckle big broom and she beltit they cockerels ower their heids so they lef' us alane. If she hadne cam' rinnin' they wouldiv pecket us to deith.

DE QUINCEY: **(laughing)** Willy! I can just picture the scene. What a breath of fresh air you are to be sure and where would I be without you my friend?

WILLY: Yid be ben the lakes.

DE QUINCEY: The lakes? Ah! The Lakes.

WILLY: That's whur yid be.

DE QUINCEY: Such peaceful surroundings. Such incomparable beauty **(He drinks more laudanum.)** Have I ever told you about the Alpine splendour of the mountains Willy?

WILLY: Aye. Yiv telt me.

DE QUINCEY: The rocky fortresses of the peaks, the spouting water tumbling down the craggy slopes into the lush and verdant valleys, the wild self-sown woodlands of birch, alder, holly, mountain ash and hazel, the elegant patchwork of the tiny fields and here and there a cluster of cottages with gentle plumes of smoke breathing up like incense to the household Gods from the simple hearths of the villagers.
'How vast the compass of this theatre,
Yet nothing to be seen but lovely pomp
And silent majesty; the birch-tree woods
Are hung with thousand thousand diamond drops
Of melted hoar-frost, every tiny knot
In the bare twigs each little budding-place
Cased with its several beads; what myriads these
Upon one tree, while all the distant grove
That rises to the summit of the steep
Shows like a mountain built of silver light
See yonder the same pageant and again
Behold the universal imagery
Inverted, all its sun-bright features touched,
As with the varnish and the gloss of dreams.'

WILLY: Cin I hae yer breid an' aw Mister . . . eh . . . ?

DE QUINCEY: My bread?

WILLY: Aye. I'm fair stervin'.

21

DE QUINCEY: No. I am afraid that you cannot Willy for I must eat as well as drink. Hunger and thirst are but brother and sister and both must be assuaged. For the time being it is my thirst that commands my greatest attention, but no doubt I shall become hungry in the course of time.

He drinks direct from the bottle.

WILLY: Aye. I c'n see yer thirsty aw richt.

DE QUINCEY: Where is the change?

WILLY: The change?

DE QUINCEY: Yes. The change,

WILLY: Thur's bin a richt hoch-colly-shangie oot at Lithgae.

DE QUINCEY: Never mind about that.

WILLY: They sodjers have aw gillygorgoned yin anither.

DE QUINCEY: Enough of your nonsense. Sixpence I think.

WILLY: Sixpence?

DE QUINCEY: Yes. The tincture is fourpence and the bread two pence. Four and two make six.

WILLY: Seven.

DE QUINCEY: Six.

WILLY: Seven.

DE QUINCEY: Six.

WILLY: Seven.

DE QUINCEY: Six. You left this room with one shilling Willy. Where is the change?

WILLY: I've lost it.

DE QUINCEY: Lost it? I do not believe you.

WILLY: 'Strue Mister . . . eh . . .

DE QUINCEY: Turn out your pockets!

WILLY: Eh?

DE QUINCEY: I said turn out your pockets!

WILLY: I wilne.

DE QUINCEY: Come along! That money is all that is left to me in the world. You surely would not deprive me of it? I shall require it for tomorrow.

WILLY: Aye. Fur mair tincture.

DE QUINCEY: You are surely not going to cheat me of it? I, who have taken you in off the street, given you shelter shared my daily bread with you. Is this how you choose to repay me Willy? With tricks and deceptions? I cannot believe it. **(Pause)** So be it. So be it. I shall suffer and starve. **(Pause. WILLY pulls a threepenny bit from his pocket.)** Three pence?

WILLY: Aye. The tincture's ten pence.

DE QUINCEY: Willy! You are such a bad liar.

WILLY: I'm no lyin!

DE QUINCEY: I require a further three pence.

WILLY: I dinnae hae it.

DE QUINCEY: What has come over you? This is not like yourself. I have never known you to be dishonest with me before. I shall obviously have to reconsider our relationship in the light of these developments. Can I ever trust you again I wonder? **(WILLY hands over three single pennies one at a time.)** One, Two. Three. There now. The matter is closed. Some things are better left unsaid. Suffice it to say that I am extremely surprised. Surprised and somewhat disappointed. We had better mention it no more. What time is it?

He searches for his watch in his pockets, cannot find it, abandons search.

WILLY: **(sulking)** Time?

DE QUINCEY: What time of the day?

WILLY: I dinnae ken.

DE QUINCEY: Is it morning or evening?

WILLY: I dinnae ken.

DE QUINCEY: Is it dark outside?

WILLY: It's aye dark.

DE QUINCEY: What! Does the sun never shine in Auld Reekie? Of course it does. In fact the very day that I arrived in this fine town the sun was shining with all its might. I had travelled by coach all through the night. I was sitting on top of the coach with the luggage, beside an enormous Scotsman whose rugged appearance had at first caused me considerable consternation. But my anxiety turned out to be totally unfounded for he was a delightful companion and whenever I fell asleep as indeed I constantly did, he would put a protective arm around my shoulder in order to save me from falling to the ground.

WILLY: He should've' let ye fa'.

DE QUINCEY: I hope that you do not mean what you say.

WILLY: Aye. I mean it aw richt.

DE QUINCEY: As we came across the Pentland Hill, there lay spread out before me in the morning sun, a magnificent spectacle which quite took my breath away. There it was – the Athens of the North – like some great grey wedding cake. How much was promised on that morning and how little has, in reality, been delivered. Ah, me! **(Pause)** I cannot forbear to ask you, Willy, why you have withheld the money from me? It is not like you to try to cheat me. For what purpose was the money intended?

WILLY: It wis fur the Kirk.

DE QUINCEY: Ah! So you were robbing the poor to give to the poor! A likely story! Tell the truth! Was it for something special to eat? Some little delicacy perhaps?

WILLY: No.

DE QUINCEY: What then?

WILLY: Fur spendin'.

DE QUINCEY: Spending?

WILLY: Aye.

DE QUINCEY: I see. And on what were you intending to spend the money?

WILLY: Eh?

DE QUINCEY: What was the money for?

WILLY: **(defiant)** Fur spendin' up the stair.

DE QUINCEY: Ah! So now we have it. The truth is out. I had feared as much. Oh, Willy! How could you? It is beyond my understanding. Surely there is nothing to be gained by venturing into that wretched place?

WILLY: Aye. There is tae.

DE QUINCEY: I cannot believe it. It is unworthy of you. I had always understood you to be a man of infinite sensibilities easily capable of overcoming the baser instincts to which the flesh is heir, but it seems I was sadly mistaken. To think that a God-fearing man like yourself should so readily yield to temptation. It shocks me to the core. You surely have your mind on higher things. Such degrading antics are beneath your dignity.

Perhaps you find me excessively harsh?

Guilty of overreaction?

After all, we all have our little peccadilloes do we not? Would not life be intolerably dull if we did not? **(He drinks.)** There now. The matter is closed. Come along old friend. Sing a song for me! Dance a Schottishe! For we are sadly in need of some entertainment. Come along!

WILLY: I willne.

DE QUINCEY: What! Do you refuse?

WILLY: Aye.

DE QUINCEY: Then it seems that I am faced with a mutiny. What should a poor Captain do under such unhappy circumstances? Quell it immediately! Arrest all the ringleaders and make them walk the plank. Or should he simply abandon ship and leave the drifting vessel to the tender mercies of the mutinous scum.

He pokes WILLY playfully.

WILLY: Away an' fuck yersel'!

DE QUINCEY: Such poverty of language is deeply offensive to me. There are so many beautiful and descriptive words in the English language. Why descend to the gutter for them when they can be plucked from a fragrant bower of the etymological garden?

WILLY: I'm gangin' awa' doon tae Leith tae throw masel' in the Clyde.

DE QUINCEY: Do not do that Willy for I have great need of you. I am sorry. For I fear I have caused you some considerable offence. What is afoot in the wide world?

WILLY: A fit?

DE QUINCEY: What sights have you seen on your travels?

WILLY: Ten inches in a fit.

DE QUINCEY: Tell me a story!

WILLY: I'll tell ye a story awricht. Are you ready?

DE QUINCEY: I am all ears.

WILLY: I can still see yer nose. Ye'll mebe no like it.

DE QUINCEY: Tell me! Tell me!

WILLY: I wis walkin' doon the Canongate when they bairns sterted efter us. Rinnin' along efter us cryin' us glaikit. But this time's a wee bitty different. There's a big laddie wi' them. Sixteen or seventeen. He telt them aw to stert throwin' stanes at us. So they aw sterted efter us throwin' their stanes. I hud tae rin fur ma life. So I rin doon a side street intae the Coogate. A roonded the corner – cock-a-doodle-doo – and there's a hale flock o' sheep comin' up the ither way. I looked ower the road to the ither side and I seen yon beggar wi' the widden leg. He had a huld o' a sheep by its wull an' he wis forcin' it, pushin' it intae a doorway. But the shepherd seen him an' he kent he wis stealin' so he shouts at the beggar tae stop wha' he's daein'. But the beggar taks nae a blind bit o' notice so the shepherd gangs across tae um and he grabs um by the lug. And he shakes um and pulls um. An' he's thrashin' um and beatin um wi' his crook when aw o' a sudden the beggar's lug comes awa' in his hon. Just like that. And there's blood spurtin' oot aw ower. Aw ower everywhere. And it taks twa or three folk tae pull the shepherd frae aff o' the beggar he wis that angry. And by this time the sheep's aff in aw differen' paerts. Up to the Pleasance an' doon Holyrood waye. So when the shepherd sees this, he leaves the beggar alane and he gangs chasin' efter the rest o' his sheep. I laupt on ma hoarse and cam' gallopin' hame.

DE QUINCEY: Willy! What a terrible tale! This is not at all what I had in mind. I wanted a story to cheer me along. Sing for me! Sing me a song for I am sorely in need of something uplifting.

WILLY: I telt ye aforehon' ye'd mebe no like it.

DE QUINCEY: Something to take my mind off the world.

WILLY: I'll sing fur ye then. Are ye ready?

DE QUINCEY: Aye.

WILLY prepares to sing. He has a surprisingly clear and melodious voice.

WILLY: **(sings)**
'The Lord is my shepherd
I'll not want
He makes me down to lie
In pastures green
He leadeth me
The quiet waters bye.

My soul he doth
Restore again
And me to walk
Doth make
Within the paths
Of righteousness
E'en for its own
Name's sake.

Goodness and mercy
All my life
Shall surely follow me
And in God's house
For ever more
My dwelling place shall be.'

Pause

DE QUINCEY: **(applauding)** Bravo! Bravo!

When I was a boy I could sing like an angel. Now I can scarcely croak. Of all the musical instruments that I have ever heard, I confess that the human voice is the most acceptable to my ears. In truth I cannot abide all that clangerous brass and the absolute tyranny of the violin I find an appalling imposition. No! Give me the human voice any day! When I was a young man I would regularly go to the Opera House in order to hear the great Grassini sing. And what a beautiful and thrilling sound wafted from the stage to the gallery whenever my beloved Guiseppina appeared in one of her famous interludes. How she poured forth her passionate soul as Andromache at the Tomb of Hector! What style was there! What miraculous melodiousness!

WILLY: I ken her. She's a whore!

DE QUINCEY: She is nothing of the kind Willy and I'll thank you to keep a civil tongue in your head. Grassini is a woman with a rare gift and an extraordinary natural charm and beauty. Some find her voice overly shrill to be, sure, but then these things are always a matter of opinion and no two critics can ever agree. The pleasure of music can be intellectual or sensual according to the temperament of the listener. For me it is one of life's supreme pleasures. Without it existence would be quite unthinkable. Music and philosophy. Ah! Philosophy.

WILLY: Aye. Richt enough.

DE QUINCEY: And in particular, German Metaphysics.

WILLY: There's a lassie in Fife wi' rabbits in her hair.

DE QUINCEY: What a miraculous creation is the extraordinary mind of Emmanuel Kant for he is indeed a veritable Copernicus among modern philosophers. Few things in the world excite me more than to explore the impenetrable thickets of his inspirational thoughts. What an astonishing insight it is to have perceived that the phenomenal world is but a picture of our own designing rather than a definitive outer experience. Up until the arrival of Kant on the scene, philosophy had concerned itself with the examination of the nature of objects rather than the perception of those objects. But the magical loom of the brain puts its own construction upon appearances. You imagine the objects in the world to be as you see them, but that is only as they appear to you. Take this room for example. When I say 'It is cold in this room', I should rather say 'It appears to me to be cold in this room' for to you it might appear to be warm.

WILLY: It doesne. It's cald aw richt.

DE QUINCEY: I speak hypothetically.

WILLY: Eh?

DE QUINCEY: Only mathematical and geometrical truths are objectively demonstrable as universal judgements and yet abstract concepts are often the result of wholly subjective intuitions. The manyfold ironies are endlessly paradoxical. Do I make myself clear?

WILLY: Aye. But there's nae use tae it.

DE QUINCEY: Never was a truer word spoken my friend! Ah! Would that I had your intellect Willy! How much simpler things would be. Are you a neo-Platonist I wonder? Or a Stoic perhaps? Or a rationalist? I rather think that you are a Stoic, believing as you do that the power of the will can control the passions and enable men to rise above pleasure and pain.

WILLY: You're a genius. So you are Mister . . . eh . . .

DE QUINCEY: Would that the world shared your opinion.

WILLY: Can I hae the rest o' the breid?

DE QUINCEY: Please help yourself for truth be told I am not inordinately hungry. Thirsty, yes. But hungry no.

He swigs more laudanum as WILLY eats.

WILLY: Is it time for the sceneries yet?

DE QUINCEY: Not yet, not yet. They cannot be forced. They must be allowed to come in their own good time. Do a dance for me Willy! Dance the Schotische!

WILLY: Here it's, here it's.

WILLY does a little dance.

DE QUINCEY: **(applauding)** Bravo! Bravo!
I used to love dancing, but now I can scarcely walk. Let us see some more of your tricks old friend.

WILLY: Here's yin ye havene' seen.
Are ye ready?

WILLY prepares himself, with great deftness he pulls from his inside pocket a fine silk handkerchief, this resembles a conjuring trick, DE QUINCEY is startled, then amused.

DE QUINCEY: Bravo! Wonderful!
For an instant I imagined that you had conjured a dove from your pocket. Where did you find it?

WILLY: It wis lyin' in the street.

DE QUINCEY: Have you been picking pockets again?

WILLY: Ye've a nose like a trumpet.

DE QUINCEY: This room is a – tilting.

WILLY: Yer ears are like cabbages.

DE QUINCEY: What is that?

WILLY: What?

DE QUINCEY: There.

WILLY: Where?

DE QUINCEY: There. On your cheek. On your cheek. Like a sprouting forest of sea anemones. Now they come upon me.

WILLY: Eh?

DE QUINCEY: Ah me! The phantoms of the eye! Help me to a chair Willy for now the sceneries are starting to unfold before me.

WILLY: There, there. Willy's here.

DE QUINCEY: Easy now old friend.
I really should not be doing this at all you know, for I have a deadline tomorrow at six o'clock. Or so I think. I should be hard at work.

WILLY: Is it time to see the sceneries yet Mister . . . eh . . . ?

DE QUINCEY: Yes indeed. I fear that it is that time. I shall now explore the darker recesses of my labyrinthine brain with the camera obscura of my mind.

WILLY: I'll go along wi' ye.

DE QUINCEY: Your devotion is touching.
Ah! What have we here? **(DE QUINCEY closes his eyes.)** There stretches before me now. in all directions, as far as the inner eye can see, a vast, open and barren plain. The only relief to the monotony of the terrain is an occasional outcrop of rock or a miserable specimen of bush. The only sound which fills the air is the plaintive music of a persistent and howling wind which serves to accentuate the forlorn and desolate nature of this pitiless place. **(WILLY imitates the sound of the wind.)** Suddenly, faintly heard from a great distance, drifting on the wind a few muffled notes of a fanfare.

(WILLY again provides this sound effect.) I turn my glance to the West and all at once, over the horizon, there appears simultaneously the gleaming tips of a thousand spears. I turn to the East and as if prompted by my glance more spears appear. I look to the North and then to the South. More shining tips! I am surrounded! Another blast on the trumpet is the signal for serried ranks of these Roman armies to advance **(WILLY obliges once more with a trumpet sound.)** and what an overwhelming spectacle they are as they move towards me, first the plumes of their golden helmets, then their crimson tunics and square-topped shields.

WILLY: Aye. I can see them!

DE QUINCEY: What an awesome sight is there!

WILLY: **(picking up the poker)** I'm ready Mister . . . eh . . . I'm ready fur them.

DE QUINCEY: They move towards me, slowly at first, in tight and disciplined formation, shoulder to shoulder, shield to shield. And then once more, on the command from the trumpet, comes the signal to charge. **(WILLY obliges.)** They lower their spears.

WILLY: I'm no afeart o' them.

DE QUINCEY: I am rooted to the spot. Where can I run to?

WILLY: There's nae need to run.

DE QUINCEY: Now they are charging, thundering forward, their spears at the ready.

WILLY: I'll fight ya! I'll kill ya!

DE QUINCEY: And now from their ranks comes a terrible yell, which turns my very blood to ice.

WILLY: **(yells)** Get back ya bastards!

DE QUINCEY: Now they are upon me. They will cut me to shreds.

WILLY: Get back ya Roman bastards!

WILLY mimes fighting.

DE QUINCEY: There is no escape! I am trapped! I am killed!

DE QUINCEY lets out a yell of terror. He opens his eyes. WILLY drops the poker and goes to comfort him.

WILLY: There. there.

DE QUINCEY: Ah!

WILLY: It's Willy.

DE QUINCEY: Where was I?

WILLY: You're aw richt.

DE QUINCEY: And the Roman armies?

WILLY: Aw gone. I seen them off.

DE QUINCEY: So lifelike! So real!
I thought that they would surely massacre me. And yet. I see now. 'Tis but a December day in 'auld reekie'.

WILLY: Aye. Let's see mair sceneries.

DE QUINCEY: What? Is there to be no respite?

WILLY: Mair sceneries!

DE QUINCEY: No. I fear not.

WILLY: Mair sceneries!

DE QUINCEY: What a cruel task master you are. Once more the curtain rises on the miniature theatre of my brain. **(He closes his eyes.)** I am floating, like a bird, above the ground.

WILLY: I can fly an aw.

He adopts a flying stance, spreading his arms.

DE QUINCEY: On a magic carpet.

WILLY: I like this yin!

DE QUINCEY: Up above voluminous clouds which heave and toss like a stormy sea. And as the clouds thin out beneath me a fabulous and rugged landscape is revealed. Great Alpine mountains capped with snow, chasms and gorges streaked with purple and orange, fabulous forests of larch and pine, and silver lakes shining like mirrors.

WILLY: Aye. I can see them!

DE QUINCEY: I soar like an eagle, and coming into view far beneath me I can see the battlements and towers of some vast and long forgotten city. Wide and spacious avenues lead off in all directions, flanked by serene pavilions encrusted with rubies and pearls.

WILLY: Can ya no get a hod o' ony o' it? You could make the baith o' us rich!

DE QUINCEY: Silver spires, alabaster domes and gorgeous palaces of deep green marble, pink minarets and elegant ballustrades.

WILLY: Aye, I can see it.

DE QUINCEY: And yet not a soul is moving in the streets. The city is deserted. Why is it deserted?

WILLY: 'Cos there's naebody there!

DE QUINCEY: It cannot be right. Perhaps there has occurred some terrible tragedy. Now I am drifting away from the city. Above the gently rocking waters of the ocean. And suddenly the surface of the sea is paved with innumerable faces, all upturned to face the Heavens. Faces imploring, wrathful, despairing, surging upwards by myriads, by generations, by centuries, by aeons. And my mind is tossed and surged with the ocean and I cannot separate myself from this infinite pageant of human misery. And my agitation is endless and my anxieties are countless. Pray rescue me from this living Hell!

WILLY shakes DE QUINCEY.

DE QUINCEY: **(opening his eyes)** Ah! Where was I?

WILLY: Flying in the air. I was flyin' wi ye.

DE QUINCEY: Had I been there long?

WILLY: Aye. Several hours.

DE QUINCEY: It seemed like an eternity.
Willy do not leave me!

WILLY: I wilne. I willne.

DE QUINCEY: I am drifting off once more. **(He closes his eyes.)**
Will it never end?

WILLY: It's only a dream,

DE QUINCEY: 'Tis a nightmare Willy. The weight of history rests heavily upon my shoulders.

WILLY: There's nothin' on yer shouders.

DE QUINCEY: I must drive my horse and cart over the bones of the dead.

WILLY: Clippety-clop, clippety-clop!

DE QUINCEY: What a perpetual torment is here. Help me to the bed pray for I am exceedingly drowsy and must extend my frail body,

WILLY: **(offering him assistance)** Here. I'll oxter ye.

DE QUINCEY: I thank you. Where am I now? 'Tis another pageant of antiquity,

WILLY: Wha' this time? Is it Robert the Bruce?

DE QUINCEY: 'Tis the ancient Greeks in all their splendour, and what a truly magnificent spectacle is here. Picture, if you will, the temple of Athena at Delphi. It is an afternoon of shimmering heat and the slopes of the mountains, thick with gnarled and ancient olive trees, slope down to the glistening blue of the Mediterranean Sea. Assembled on the steps, around the stately columns of the temple, is a large and excitable multitude hushed in expectation. From an invisible stairway there suddenly emerges a solemn procession of chanting priestesses. **(WILLY beats out a rhythm.)** They move to form a circle. The crowd presses forward. At the centre of the circle, there rises up a thin blue column of smoke. The rhythm of the drumbeat changes. The priestesses start to dance and sway, slowly at first, then faster and faster. Then one of the priestesses fetches a basket, a basket full of laurel leaves. She casts the leaves upon the fire. The smokes begins to thicken. Still chanting rhythmically they move forward, inhaling the fumes, gulping in the intoxicating smoke. The drumbeat quickens yet again. The dancing is becoming more frenzied and more frantic. The priestesses spin and weave.

WILLY: Spin and weave.

DE QUINCEY: Like demented tops!
  Now they are tearing at their clothes.

WILLY: Cock-a-doodle-do!

DE QUINCEY: Shaking ecstatically.

WILLY: Hoyte-oy-ty-oy!

DE QUINCEY: The crowd surges forward like a wild animal.

WILLY: Like a wild animal!

DE QUINCEY: The drumbeat deafens.

The priestesses scream in orgiastic frenzy.

WILLY: They're aw sterk naked!

DE QUINCEY: The crowd is possessed.

Then, like a single being it hurtles down the mountain like the Gadarene swine and plunges its demonic self into the foaming Mediterranean. And the sea turns from blue to red as the water is flooded with its sacrificial blood. Peace! No more!

WILLY: Where to now Mister . . . eh . . . ?

DE QUINCEY: Let us enter the strange world of Signor Piranesi. I see vast gothic halls. And on the floors of these halls stand engines and machinery, wheels, cables, pulleys, levers and catapults, expressing great power put forth and resistance overcome.

WILLY makes creaks and clanking noises.

DE QUINCEY: And now I see a staircase, and there upon it, groping his way upwards, is Signor Piranesi himself. But wait! For if you follow the staircase a little further forward it comes to an abrupt end with only the depths below. He is going to fall. I know that he is going to fall! And then, as if by magic, another flight of steps appears, and Piranesi walks on upwards. Onwards up the stairs.

WILLY: Aye. On up the stair!

DE QUINCEY: Again it appears to end, but just in time another flight. Still higher, then still higher.

WILLY: I must go an' aw.

DE QUINCEY: Endless growth. Self-replication.

On, on. Up, up.

WILLY: I'll dae what ye tell me.

WILLY goes to the bed where DE QUINCEY is lying. He removes the money from DE QUINCEY'S pocket.

DE QUINCEY: Another flight. Another stairway. (**WILLY leaves the room.**) On, on! Up, up! No balustrade. He is going to fall. Still more. Still higher. What have we here? The Day of Judgement? A day of ultimate crisis? I know not what. I know not where. I hear the tread of marching armies. I see infinite cavalcades, hurryings to and fro, trepidations of frightened fugitives carrying with them all their worldly possessions. There has been a battle, a strife, an agony. I know not why. I know not where. Darkness and light, storms and tempests, female forms sobbing and weeping, clasped hands, thunder and lightening, heartbreaking partings, everlasting farewells. And now there comes an enormous explosion, a ball of fire, a shower of sparks, a sheet of flame and an end to all that is living and breathing.

There is a great commotion on the stairway outside the room. Voices raised in anger. An almighty crash as WILLY is pushed down the stairs. A long silence. Groaning from outside the door. The door opens slowly. WILLY crawls in on all fours his face is covered with blood. He crawls towards DE QUINCEY. DE QUINCEY opens his eyes. He sees WILLY'S bloodstained face but is unsure as to whether it is a hallucination or not. He touches WILLY'S face. He has blood on his fingers. He realises that this is not a vision. He screams in horror. Blackout.

Act 2

Scene 1

The same, ten minutes later. WILLY is on the bed. The shock of the accident has brought DE QUINCEY round. He makes a valiant attempt to cope.

WILLY: I'm sorry Mister . . . eh . . .

DE QUINCEY: There, there.

WILLY: I'm gey sorry.

DE QUINCEY: Keep calm!

WILLY: Ah! Mercy me.

DE QUINCEY: Lie still!

WILLY: May God have mercy upon ma soul.

DE QUINCEY: Where is the pain?

WILLY: Here. In ma back,

DE QUINCEY: Where?

WILLY: Fair torturin' me.

DE QUINCEY: You must show me the precise location.

WILLY: Eh?

DE QUINCEY: Where exactly?

WILLY: Ah! Mercy me! I canne move.

DE QUINCEY: Let us hope that there are no bones broken.

WILLY: I'm sorry Mister . . . eh . . .

DE QUINCEY: No need to apologise. We must find the source of your discomfort. Please turn over.

WILLY: Ah!

DE QUINCEY: That is it.

WILLY: Ah!

DE QUINCEY: Now tell me if I am causing you pain. **(He prods.)**

WILLY: Aye!

DE QUINCEY: Here?

WILLY: Aye!

DE QUINCEY: Here? Clearly all is not well with you. How came this about?

WILLY: They pushed me doon.

DE QUINCEY: Who pushed you Willy?

WILLY: They pushed me backward.

DE QUINCEY: Who did?

WILLY: They men up the stair.

DE QUINCEY: Upstairs?

WILLY: Aye. Up the stair.

DE QUINCEY: Ah, So. You have ventured into the forbidden land. Did you fall all the way? From the top to the bottom?

WILLY: Aye. Aw the way doon. I rolled ower an' ower. Oh Jeesis save me!

DE QUINCEY: I am heartily sorry but I cannot imagine what on earth can have possessed you to enter into that sorry place.

WILLY: Ye telt me tae go.

DE QUINCEY: I beg your pardon?

WILLY: Ye telt me tae go.

DE QUINCEY: What? Am I hearing aright?

WILLY: Ye did tae. 'Strue. 'Up the stair' ye said. 'Gang on up the stair'.

DE QUINCEY: Surely you are mistaken.

WILLY: 'Strue, I'm tellin' ye. 'Strue.

DE QUINCEY: Then I can only think that I must have been dreaming. For my part, it is the last place on earth that I should have wished you to go. Such a sordid scene of human degradation! I do not know whether 'tis the whores who are the more to be pitied or their wretched clients. Why some of those poor little creatures seem scarcely to be out of their cradles. What on God's earth can have induced you to visit?

WILLY: Ya telt me tae go. I felt like it an' aw.

DE QUINCEY: You felt like it?

WILLY: Aye. I felt like a thrashing.

DE QUINCEY: The matter is beyond my comprehension.

WILLY: I wis efter a thrashing

DE QUINCEY: A thrashing?

WILLY: Aye.

DE QUINCEY: Then it seems you have been successful in achieving your goal.

WILLY: No like that. Wi' a stick. Frae a lassie.

DE QUINCEY: Stranger and stranger. May one enquire as to the reason for this?

WILLY: Gie's us the hornie.

DE QUINCEY: The hornie Willy?

WILLY: Aye. **(WILLY gestures.)**

DE QUINCEY: You poor creature. I pity you from the very depths of my being. I have known of course that you have wanted to visit the brothel for some considerable time. I have had my suspicions about this strange inclination and have not been entirely oblivious to the fact that to some extent you are inevitably at the mercy of your baser appetites but I never thought to see the day when such a vile transgression would become an actuality.

WILLY: Ah! Mercy me! **(He cries out in pain.)**

DE QUINCEY: Come old friend! You must pull yourself together,

WILLY: Ma pair back.

DE QUINCEY: Lie still. There, there.
Far be it for me to delve into what has already passed, but there is something I feel I must ask of you, Willy, out of a sense of duty. I feel I must ask you to tell me exactly what took place from the moment that you left this room.

WILLY: I went up the stair. I went in ben the door. There were twa lassies sittin' there. Yin o' them had a shawl roond her shouders. The ither yin had goose fithers in her hair. **(Pause)**

DE QUINCEY: Yes. Proceed!

WILLY: So I esked yin o' them tae gi' us a thrashin'. They baith sterted laughin' at us. Then yin o' them went oot the door. I thought mebe she wis awa fur a whip. The yin with the fithers telt us to sit doon. So I din whit she says. She sterted eskin' us aw kinds o' things. Had I bin in afore. Where wis I frae. Wis I merried or single. Then the ither yin-came back wi' twa big bulls o' men. Aw o' a sudden yin o' them pult ma airms behind us. I tried tae fight wi' him and I kicked him on the ankle but he held us doon and the ither yin went intae ma pockets. Then the twa o' them pulled us tae the dare and they pushed us

43

doon the stair. Oh. mercy me!

DE QUINCEY: What a very distressing story! But there is one small crumb of comfort. At least all your pockets were mercifully empty

WILLY: Oh dearie me! I can hairdly bring masel' tae tell ye. Ma pockets wurnae empty.

DE QUINCEY: What?

DE QUINCEY checks his pockets. Finds them all to be empty.

DE QUINCEY: Nothing! Then you have stolen from me. Are there no depths to which you will not descend?

WILLY: I'm gey sorry.

DE QUINCEY: I never thought to see you sink so low.

WILLY: I didne mean tae.

DE QUINCEY: Such behaviour is utterly unpardonable.

WILLY: It jist haeppent.

DE QUINCEY: It is the very devil himself who has taken possession of your soul.

WiLLY: Oh Jeesis save me! Ma per back. I canna tak muckle mer o' it.

DE QUINCEY: What an unutterable fool you have been.

WILLY: Ma back!

DE QUINCEY: Here. You must drink some of this.

WILLY: No!

DE QUINCEY: 'Tis the only solution.

WILLY: I willne.

DE QUINCEY: You must. It will quell the pain.

WILLY: I willne.

DE QUINCEY: Drink it!

WILLY: Dinna mak us.

DE QUINCEY: Why do you refuse? It will quell the pain.

WILLY: I'm feart o' it.

DE QUINCEY: Feart?

WILLY: Aye, I'm feart o' the sceneries. I'm feart o' seein' they sceneries. I'm feart o' seein' they Romins. I'm feart o' seein' aw they dungeons an' dragins. There's no mony things that I'm no affeart o'.

DE QUINCEY: Your fear is understandable, but such a small quantity of the tincture as I propose to administer would have no such dramatic effect. The soothing properties of the laudanum would be most beneficial. In fact it is highly likely that you will see nothing at all. Dreamless sleep is the likeliest outcome. And even if your dreams were to be visionary in character it is unlikely that their contents would bear any relation to the violence and cruelty of my tormented imaginings. The mind is but a blank sheet of paper on which is writ all past experience. Nothing is ever erased although it may be forgotten. It is imprinted forever, a lasting testament to the past. My visions are but the product of my reading and my learning. They are devised from pictures I have seen in history books or stories I have read as a child which are inscribed forever in the archives of my memory. Your pictures would be of an entirely different order. Scenes of childhood. Remembrances of the manse. Country and woodland. Mountain and lake.

WILLY: Loch.

DE QUINCEY: Forgive me. Loch.
Pray reconsider. It will relieve you of your misery.

He holds out the bottle. A pause. WILLY raises his arm. A cry of pain.

WILLY: Jeesis save me!

DE QUINCEY: There, there. Please allow me.
Greater love hath no man.

He lifts the bottle to WILLY'S lips. WILLY drinks cautiously. He licks his lips.

WILLY: It tastes like Kirkcoobri'.

DE QUINCEY: Kirkcudbright Willy? And how does Kirkcudbright taste?

WILLY: Bonny. Like persley. Can I hae a wee drap mair?

DE QUINCEY: Yes I suppose you must. For so very little is unlikely to be effective. **(WILLY drinks again.)** That will suffice. Give it back to me please!

WILLY: I willne.

DE QUINCEY: Why must you always exasperate me so and drive me to the very brink of distraction. Give it back to me! **(WILLY drinks the remainder of the bottle.)** You did that deliberately. Odious creature. I hope you are satisfied with your spiteful work. First of all you succeed is getting rid of all that remains of my worldly wealth and now you have finished the last precious drops of my beloved laudanum. Look! See! Empty! No laundamun, no money, no nothing! Do you want to know something? I am glad that your back is giving you such pain! I sincerely hope that the discomfort remains acute! May the pain of a thousand red hot pokers be visited upon your spine forever!

WILLY: Ah! Mercy me!

DE QUINCEY: I did not mean it! I got carried away. How are we to extricate ourselves from this perilous situation? Perhaps I should walk directly up the stairs and demand the return of the money forthwith. An Oxford education generally does the trick. **(Brutal shout from above.)** But in this particular instance, I fear that it might count for nothing.

WILLY: They'd murder ye.

DE QUINCEY: Thank you indeed for inspiring such confidence. A great help you are I must say! Perhaps you could suggest a suitable remedy? After all, it is you who has got us into this fine mess.

WILLY: You'll hae tae feenish yer story.

DE QUINCEY: The story?

WILLY: Aye. Fur Blackwood. Ten poond ye said.

DE QUINCEY: Ah! That is easier said than done. For I am somewhat bereft of inspiration and have nothing left to write.

WILLY: There's plenty o' things,

DE QUINCEY: Oh. What sort of things?

WILLY: You could write aboot me.

DE QUINCEY: I could indeed, but I fear that I would not be believed.

WILLY: You could write about Chrismis.

DE QUINCEY: Hardly relevant. My essay is entitled Confessions of an English Opium Eater.

WILLY: Aye, weil, you could write aboot the tincture. Aw aboot the tincture.

DE QUINCEY: I have already done so.

WILLY: You could write aboot the sceneries. Aw aboot the sceneries.

DE QUINCEY: The sceneries?

WILLY: Aye. You could write your dream sceneries.

DE QUINCEY: I think that you might have something there Willy.

WILLY: Aye. A sair back.

DE QUINCEY: Something of substance. But would the public at large be interested I wonder?

WILLY: Aye. They would tae.

DE QUINCEY: You think so?

WILLY: I dae tae.

DE QUINCEY: It seems to me that it would be worth a try. It is an excellent idea and I am indebted to you for it. I shall begin forthwith. Clear the decks! Where is my quill? Pray quiet upstairs! I must have quiet! Some hope of that. Now, where was I? Yes let me see. I shall describe the substance of my dreams.
(Writing)
'I now pass to what is the main subject of these latter confessions, to the history and journal of what took place in my dreams.'
Willy, you are a genius.

WILLY: Aye. I ken. I telt them in the skull but they didne believe us.

DE QUINCEY writes on as the lights fade.

Scene 2

A few hours later. DE QUINCEY works. WILLY is in a state of delirium. He sleeps restlessly and mumbles incoherently.

DE QUINCEY: **(writing and reading out loud as he does so)**
'My sleep is still tumultuous, and, like the gates of Paradise to our first parents when looking back from afar, it is still, in the tremendous line of Milton' – acknowledge the source, acknowledge the source – 'with dreadful faces thronged and fiery arms'. **(A groan from WILLY.)** There. 'Tis done. What a blessed relief. What a burden is lifted from my mind! What of the quality? Will it suffice? Is there perhaps too little humour? Or too much. Too little substance? Or too much.

WILLY: Willy's a way, way up a kaie.

DE QUINCEY: Have I buried my meaning too deeply
Or made it too obvious.
What will the critics make of it I wonder?
Better than the last one. But not as good as the one before that.
'Mister De Quincey persists with his unfortunate tendency towards the grossest forms of self-indulgence.'
'Mister De Quincey sometimes seems more interested in the sound of the words than in their meaning.'
'Mister De Quincey's style is adequate but his thoughts are very muddled.'

WILLY: See they moles on the fence.
I've eaten thame afore noo.

DE QUINCEY: Heaven alone knows what Mister Blackwood will make of the more exotic passages.
(In a Scottish accent.)
'To be perfectly candid Mister De Quincey I find your essay so much pie in the sky. Could you not concentrate on real issues for a change? An article for instance, on the fisherfolk of Leith would be most warmly welcomed. Or something dealing with the important issue of eighteenth century settlement in the Highland glens. But this subject is of strictly limited interest to a minority audience. Leave metaphysics to the philosophers. The general public wants something it can really get its teeth

into. Something it can recognise. Something to relate to. In short, real life, Mister De Quincey, as opposed to the fantastical meanderings of a drug-ridden imagination.'

WILLY: Wee Willy Winkey ran thro' the toon.

DE QUINCEY: If only he could see how real it was to me. I must get the work to his office and ten pounds will be my reward. But how am I to get it there? My messenger is temporarily indisposed. I wonder, should I rouse him from his torpor? No. I will let him rest. In his present condition he would be of little use. I could perhaps send the work by sedan chair. Make Blackwood pay on receipt. But what if he should refuse? The work would surely go astray. Or blow away! Weeks of toil scattered to the four winds.

WILLY: See you broon rat chasin' efter us?

DE QUINCEY: The risk is too great.

WILLY: It's crawlin' wi' flees.

DE QUINCEY: I have no choice. I must venture from this room under my own volition, a prospect which fills my heart with fear and trepidation. And yet where is the difficulty in that? All that is required is the placing of one foot directly in front of the other. Nothing could be easier than that. Look. See.
(He demonstrates. He moves towards the door. Stops.)
But in which direction should my footsteps lead me? Now let me see. Blackwoods. That is in Princes Street. Up to the High Street. Down the Earthen Mound. First on the right, then second on the left. No, no. That's wrong. There is a quicker way. Straight down the High Street. Left at the bottom then left again and second on the right. No, no! That is wrong too. I should aim for Castle Terrace. Down behind the castle, then into Princes Street. No! That is wrong too.
The answer is to ask. Ask someone in the street, Nothing could be easier.

(He moves towards the door. Stops.)
But what a terrifying prospect is there here for me. I must approach a complete and utter stranger in the street and I must speak to him or her. And I must demand a question of that person. And I must solicit a response which in all probability will be totally incomprehensible to me.

WILLY: That's no ma mither there!

DE QUINCEY: If I approach a man he will undoubtedly turn out to be a murderer. Or worse.

WILLY: That's Mary the mither o' Jesus!

DE QUINCEY: If I approach a lady she will undoubtedly turn out to be a whore. Or worse. Some granite featured landlady to whom through no fault of my own I have had occasion to find myself most regrettably in considerable financial arrears. 'Tis not a pretty prospect. And yet I must do it.
(He moves towards the door. Stops.)
Perhaps there lurks somewhere a shadowy figure lying in wait in some close or wynd. A cut-throat, vagabond or thief, waiting to pounce like a fiend from hell, a bedraggled desperado who is unfortunate enough to imagine that I, of all people, am a man of some substance. Perhaps even now he skulks in the shadows waiting for his defenceless prey. Agh! 'Tis too horrible to contemplate! I will not venture out. And yet for the sake of the money I must do it.
(He goes to the door, puts his hand on the door knob. Stops.)
What if there should chance to come a gust of wind which should cause to fall a slate or chimney pot? And what if that slate or chimney pot should chance to fall directly upon my unprotected head? What then?
(He listens.)
But there is no wind. I hear no wind.

WILLY: There's naethin' in ma pocket.

DE QUINCEY: What if there should chance to be some near invisible pot hole in the cobbled street?

WILLY: It's empty I'm tellin' ye. There's naethin' there,

DE QUINCEY: A gaping void, like a Tiger Trap, ready to swallow me up. You must use your eyes to avoid such pitfalls. Perhaps a tree will blow across the road. There are not many trees in this neck of the woods.
(He goes to the door. Stops.)
What if there should chance to come a bolt of lightening? I had a cousin once who was struck by lightening. What a hideous death, to be burned alive. But see how my fancy runs away with me. It is far too cold for thunder and lightening.

WILLY: Ye canna see into it. No frae where you're sittin' ony road.

DE QUINCEY moves to the door. Puts his hand on the knob.

DE QUINCEY: I have heard it said that Arthur's Seat was once volcanic. Could it not be so again? A fullscale eruption of molten larva would certainly put paid to my immediate prospects. But then there is no defence against such devastation and one is equally as vulnerable indoors as out.

WILLY: Let's hae a look intae that pocket then.

DE QUINCEY: Earthquakes are unheard of in these parts

WILLY: Come on. Open up.

DE QUINCEY: Up to this time. A cosmic collision is a possibility. A planet frying off course or a meteorite. Or a sudden tilting of the earth's axis.

WILLY: Doon a bit mair.

DE QUINCEY: The potential for disasters seems unlimited. Being alive is a constant risk.

WILLY: Doon a bit mair.

DE QUINCEY: I must simply take my life in my hands and hope that my work is not a literary disaster.
(He goes to the door, puts his hand on the knob. Stops.)
What if I should return to find that the door is barred against me? But how could that come about, Willy could not do it. He is incapacitated. Should I leave him alone I wonder? Yes. Why not. Now. One, two, three. Go! First refusal. Try again. One, two. three. Go!
(He finally exits. A short pause. He returns.)
I have forgotten my overcoat. I cannot part without my overcoat.
(He picks up his coat. Puts it on. Exits.)

WILLY: What have we here? A sheet of pure silk? That's worth ten poond.

DE QUINCEY re-enters.

DE QUINCEY: My neckerchief. I have forgotten my neckerchief. I will be cold without it.

He exits.

WILLY: What's this? A silver spoon.

DE QUINCEY re-enters.

DE QUINCEY: My hat. I have gone without my hat

He exits.

WILLY: What's this? A golden goose.

DE QUINCEY re-enters.

DE QUINCEY: I have forgot the purpose of my perilous journey. I have forgot my essay. One day I fear I may forget my wits.

He exits.

WILLY: Gold. Pure gold. That's worth a hundred poond.

He laughs in his sleep.

Scene 3

Two hours later. WILLY lies in bed inert, his eyes open. The delirium has passed. After a few moments, DE QUINCEY bursts into the room. He is very distraught and breathless.

DE QUINCEY: Pray let me be seated for I am run ragged! All round the Town! May God give me strength! I fear that an attack of the vapours may be imminent. **(He sits.)** Ah me! Here is a fine kettle of fish.

WILLY: Eh?

DE QUINCEY: Something has occurred worse even than my wildest imaginings, beyond the realms of my blackest nightmares. Something so terrible that hellfire itself seems positively welcoming by comparison. I have arrived too late for the magazine. It has already gone to the printers.

WILLY: Eh?

DE QUINCEY: The deadline has come and gone.

WILLY: Cock-a-doodle-do!

DE QUINCEY: I am glad that you can be so flippant, my friend, but once the hunger starts to gnaw and nibble at your entrails you will surely start to sing a very different song.

WILLY: I'll no sing onything onymair.

DE QUINCEY: Did you not tell me that it was Friday today? Friday you said. As it happens you could not have been more mistaken. It is Monday today Willy. Monday. All day. I was fully two days late for Mister Blackwood's magazine. What a fool I felt! What an absolute fool! I shall suffer for this to be sure.

WILLY: You could aye gi' it tae King James.

DE QUINCEY: A fine help you are I must say. To be perfectly candid I have never considered the magazine to be of a particularly high standard. As a matter of fact, I much prefer Tait's. Or even the London Magazine. The occasional article in Blackwood's is interesting but there is generally little of any significance and one must wade through oceans of dross to find it. Without my vivid contribution it will appear lacklustre indeed. Serves him right. **(In a Scottish accent)** 'I am sorry Misteer De Quincey but it appears that you cannot be relied upon to produce on time.' To produce on time? What does he think I am? A pregnant cow that I may somehow calf whenever Mister Blackwood deems it appropriate.
What a tragedy is here Willy!
What a vile occurrence!
What a monumental calamity that I should sink so low!
Now the clouds of despair hang heavily about my head and the blackness of the situation is all pervasive!
Now my humiliation is complete and all is turned to dust and bitterest gall!

He sobs and shakes.

WILLY: Yer a genius. So ye are Mister . . . eh . . .

DE QUINCEY: I thank you.

WILLY: 'Strue.

DE QUINCEY: Such abiding faith in me is touching. But forgive me Willy for in my preoccupied state I had quite forgot your own difficulties. How fares your back?

WILLY: Still sair.

DE QUINCEY: And will be so, I fear for some considerable time to come. Oh Willy! What is to become of us for now we are truly penniless?

WILLY: We could aye rob the mail coach.

DE QUINCEY: What a spectacle would be there! How the coach driver would tremble in his boots at the sight of such a formidable pair! A disabled simpleton and an enfeebled opium addict. I doubt we would even dent his topcoat. I am sorry, Willy, I did not mean that, but I cannot see that we would make any kind of a success out of crime.
Is there any bread remaining?

WILLY: I feenished it afore.
I'm sorry Mister . . . eh . . .
Mebe I'll gang oot tae Ma Spittals. It's bakin' day the day.
I'll try tae git up.

He does so.

DE QUINCEY: No, no! Lie still!

WILLY: I'll mebe gang oot fir the beggin'.

DE QUINCEY: You must rest! I insist! Lie still! Do not move!

WILLY: I canna onyroad,

DE QUINCEY: Good, I am glad.

WILLY: Ye could try it yersel'.

DE QUINCEY: Try what?

WILLY: Try the beggin'.

DE QUINCEY: Begging? No, never. I could never stoop to begging.

WILLY: There nae need for stoopin'. Standin's aw right. There's naethin wrong wi' a wee bit honest beggin'. You could try it fur yersel'. First ye hae tae pick oot the richt kinda folk. Folk wi' bairns is best. Twa men taegither's nae good at aw. Ye've tae gang up wi' style an' no aw fearty. Walk straight up an' no roond the back. If you gang roond the back ye'll mebe gey a fright. Then speak wi' a clear voice; 'Can ye no spare a penny fur a pere sowel in need o' somethin' tae eat.' Wid ye like to hae a try?

DE QUINCEY: I do not think that I would (**He starts to shiver.**) O miserere! Now the pains begin.

WILLY: Ye've nae telt us aboot the lakes the day. Can you no tell us aw aboot the lakes.

DE QUINCEY: The lakes? Ah. yes, the lakes.

DE QUINCEY shivers intermittently throughout the following speech. There is a tension between the physical pain of withdrawal and the pleasure of remembrance.

DE QUINCEY: Let there be a cottage standing in a valley eighteen miles from any town – no spacious valley, but about two miles long by three quarters of a mile in average width, let the mountains be real mountains between three and four thousand feet high, and the cottage is a real cottage not, as a witty author has it 'a cottage with a double coach-house'. Let it be in fact – for I must abide by the actual scene – a white cottage, with flowering shrubs, so chosen as to unfold a succession of blooms upon the walls, and clustering around the windows, through all the months of Spring, Summer and Autumn – beginning in fact with May roses and ending with jasmine. Let it, however, not be Spring but Winter in his sternest shape. For surely everybody is aware of the divine pleasures which attend a winter fireside. Candles at four o'clock, warm hearth rugs, tea, a fair tea-maker, shutters closed, curtains flowing in ample draperies on the floor, whilst the wind-and rain are raging audibly without.

Paint me, then, a room seventeen feet by twelve, and not more than seven and a half feet high. This room is somewhat ambitiously styled, the drawing room, but it is also and more justly termed the library for it happens that books are the only article of property in which I am richer than my neighbours. Of these, I have about five thousand collected gradually since my eighteenth year. And the next article brought forward should naturally be myself – a picture of the opium eater with his little golden receptacle of the pernicious drug lying beside him on the table. As to the opium, I have no objection to see a picture of that, though I would rather see the original, but you may paint it if you choose but I apprize you that no little receptacle would answer my purpose. You may as well paint the receptacle as much like a wine decanter as possible. Into this you may put a quart of ruby coloured laudanum. That, and a book of German metaphysics placed by its side, will sufficiently attest my being in the neighbourhood. But as to myself – there I demur.

But now farewell – a long farewell to happiness – winter or summer! Farewell to smiles and laughter. Farewell to peace of mind. Farewell to hope and to tranquil dreams and to the blessed consolations of sleep for I am now arrived at an Iliad of woes.
Willy? Are you asleep?

WILLY: Aye. I'm asleep.

DE QUINCEY: I wish that I had never been born. Can you understand that feeling?

WILLY: Aye.

DE QUINCEY: And you feel like that yourself?

WILLY: Aye. Aw o' the time.

DE QUINCEY: What is to become of us?

WILLY: Ye've got a face like Warr'ston Ceemetary Mister . . .eh . . .

Slow fade.

Scene 4

DE QUINCEY is shivering and shaking severely.

WILLY: Did you know I was a member of the Royal Scottish Horticultural Society Mister . . . eh . . . ? 'Strue. I was knighted an' aw. In seeventeen-seeventy-sux. I've bin at the bar fur twa years noo but I've neever seen a case like this afore. I've neever had a case like this. **(Pause)** Is it the fever, eh? Eh?

DE QUINCEY: Is what the fever?

WILLY: Is it the fever that's troublin' ye?

DE QUINCEY: There is nothing that troubles me.

WILLY: Nae doubt you'll be wantin' yer ane beddy back. Ye should lie doon mebe.

DE QUINCEY: I am perfectly happy where I am.

WILLY: Aye. I can tell. Yin day I was drawin' on a pavin' stane wi' a bit o' burnt stick when this auld wummin come ridin' along in a coach. She telt us tae get in wi' her an' she taks us back to her hoose an' gies us a big lump o' cheese. Then efter I'd feenished she gies us a kitten. A wee kitten in a sack. She telt us it needed droonin'. So I took the wee sowel doon tae the burn and I helt it under the watter and I droont it. I went back to the hoose but she's aw ready awa. She's awready awa tae Dundee. So I left the hoose an' I came back hame.

DE QUINCEY: Fascinating!

WILLY: Whit's the maitter wi' ye? Ye're gey crabbit the day.

DE QUINCEY: I am not in the mood for ghoulish stories, though God knows my own is ghoulish enough.

WILLY: Shall I sing ye a song?

DE QUINCEY: You must do as you please.

WILLY: Why are ye shakin'?

Pause

DE QUINCEY: I have decided that I must leave Edinburgh,

WILLY: Eh?

DE QUINCEY: I must leave Edinburgh.

WILLY: Oh.

DE QUINCEY: There is nothing here for me anymore. I have no alternative but to return to the cottage.

WILLY: Whit's that yer saying?

DE QUINCEY: I must go back to the lakes. Perhaps London will be more kindly disposed to my 'confessions'.

WILLY: So yer gangin' awa?

DE QUINCEY: Yes.

WILY: I dinna believe it.

DE QUINCEY: It is true. I must.

WILLY: I canna believe it.

How will ye traivel? Ye've nae mair mony?

DE QUINCEY: I shall simply have to borrow from a friend. I am sure that Mister Wilson will advance me something. He has always been very good to me in the past.

WILLY: Aye, weil, its awricht fur some.

DE QUINCEY: What do you mean?

WILLY: Whit aboot us?

DE QUINCEY: You Willy?

WILLY: Aye. Me. Whits tae become o' me?

DE QUINCEY: You can stay here, for a few days at any rate. The rent is paid up until the end of the week.

WILLY: The end o' the week?

DE QUINCEY: Yes.

WILLY: And whit then?

DE QUINCEY: Your back will soon heal, then your life will go on much as it did before. You have many friends. You will survive just as you have always survived.

WILLY: I'll be terrible lonely.

DE QUINCEY: We are all on our own in this world.

WILLY: So it's back tae the workhoose fur Willy? I canna bide it. It's an awfy place. They beat ye ower the knuckles and they poke ye in the ribs aw the time. You canna leave Ed'nbrugh Mister . . . eh . . . It's mair than a pair sowel can ston'. Ye canna leave.

DE QUINCEY: I can and I must.

WILLY: I'll come wi 'ye.

DE QUINCEY: How could you Willy?

WILLY: I'll come wi' ye tae the lakes.

DE QUINCEY: No, Willy, no!

WILLY: I'll be nae bother. Nae bother at aw. I'll run the messeges for ye. I'll fetch yer tincture. I'll sing and donce fur ye.

OE QUINCEY: It just would not work.

WILLY: Then I canne survive. I'll sterve tae deith. I'll kill masel' so I will.

WILLY sobs throughout DE QUINCEY'S speech.

DE QUINCEY: Why must you torture me so? You have already lived through some forty summers or so I should guess. Why not forty more? After all, it is only a matter of a few short weeks since first we met. Do you remember our first meeting? We were standing outside Hollyrood House. You came up to me and you asked me if I was interested in riding in your hansom cab. When I replied in the affirmative you disappeared and returned a few minutes later with a lantern. Then you opened the door of the lantern and invited me to climb inside. You certainly succeeded in cheering me considerably on that fateful day. And on others since then. Come along, old friend, there is no need for that.

WILLY: Whit's to become' o' us?

DE QUINCEY: There is a coach departing sometime today. I must attempt to be on it. If I start out today I should be there by Thursday. Where is my trunk?

WILLY: Unner the bed.

DE QUINCEY pulls out a metal trunk.

DE QUINCEY: I must take some of my books with me. And of

course my essay. The papers are yours to do with as you will.

WILLY: Where's the use in thame?

DE QUINCEY: They may be very valuable one day. Part of the heritage of English Literature.

WILLY: Aye, They'll be useful . . . fur wipin' ma erse'.

DE QUINCEY: Do not speak so crudely!

WILLY: I'll mak a muckle bonfire oot in the close. Burn the lot o' them. Then burn masel' tae.

More sobbing.

DE QUINCEY: Please do not make this matter any more difficult than it already is. You must be aware of the suffering you are causing. I fear that I have created a false sense of expectation and that I am unable to fulfil my responsibilities. Oh Willy do not subject me to the rack for I fear that my feeble frame will disintegrate. Let us not part antagonistically. Come now old friend.

WILLY: Yer gangin' awa?

DE QUINCEY: Yes.

WILLY: I canna believe it.

DE QUINCEY: Say goodbye to me civilly!

WILLY: Ah! Ma pair back.

DE QUINCEY: Farewell old friend.

They embrace. WILLY does not let go. DE QUINCEY struggles to remove WILLY'S embrace.

WILLY: Cock-a-doodle-do Mister De Courcie. Cock-a-doodle-do.

DE QUINCEY: Goodbye old friend. I only hope that I shall reach my destination.

WILLY: Ye'll dae that awricht.

DE QUINCEY: Farewell.

DE QUINCEY exits dragging his trunk behind him. Pause. He re-enters.

DE QUINCEY: I have forgotten my essay. Farewell.

He exits. WILLY rises slowly from the bed. He looks around the room. He moves to the writing table and sits down. He imitates DE QUINCEY.

WILLY: Aw they wee curlies in rows and rows. Willy dae writin' tae.
(He stands and moves to centre.)
Willy's awricht.
(He goes into the inner pocket of his overcoat and produces like a conjurer, a piece of lace.)
Here's a fine piece o' lace tae cherm a lassie wi'.
(He produces a silver spoon.)
Here's plenty money frae the broker's office.
(He produces a gold watch and chain.)
Here's mutton pie and tattes fur the rest o' the year.
Cock-a-doodle-do Mister De Courcie. Cock-a-doodle-do.

He launches into a triumphal dance as the lights fade.

End

Oedipus The Visionary

David Greig

David Greig's fine adaptation produces a clarity of narrative and a simple, resonant language that renders the epic accessible.

Robert Thomson, Herald

. . . an incisive exploration of the relationship between character and fate.

Sue Wilson, Independent

ISBN 0-9549625-1-6

£8.99

Available from Booksource
Tel: +44(0)8702 402 182 Fax: +44(0)1415 570 189
email: customerservices@booksource.net

Web orders at www.capercailliebooks.co.uk

Dissent

Stephen Greenhorn

Greenhorn has penned a sharp comedy that looks at the government from a very different angle . . . Dissent does not dwell on the personalities of New Labour but focuses on the motives that drive politicians up the greasy pole. The play fires a broadside at the new generation of pragmatists whom the electoral landslide brought to power . . . What Dissent does very successfully is dramatise the process by which grassroots support is traded for influence inside the party.

The Guardian

ISBN 0-9545206-9-6

£8.99

Available from Booksource
Tel: +44(0)8702 402 182 Fax: +44(0)1415 570 189
email: customerservices@booksource.net

Web orders at www.capercailliebooks.co.uk

The Salt Wound

Stephen Greenhorn

The Salt Wound ushers in not only the monumental sea but also an almost oppressive awareness of a close-knit fishing community with all its orthodoxies, traditions and celebrations. Greenhorn does a convincing job of taking the classical passions of Greek tragedy and transposing them to a modern setting. Everyone is right and wrong. No-one can do anything about it . . . It holds an audience gripped.

The Glasgow Herald

ISBN 09549625-0-8

£8.99

Available from Booksource
Tel: +44(0)8702 402 182 Fax: +44(0) 1415 570 189
email: customerservices@booksource.net

Web orders at www.capercailliebooks.co.uk

Electra

Tom McGrath

As a dramatist, Tom McGrath's great strength is to pare things down to the fewest possible words, the sparsest settings, only the most elemental action. This piece zings with more compressed meaning than many ten times its length. It resonates powerfully for all of us watching similar stories unfolding in the Middle East, Congo, Rwanda, the USA and Northern Ireland.

Bob Tait, Theatre Reviewer and Literary Critic

ISBN 0-9549625-2-4

£8.99

Available from Booksource
Tel: +44(0)8702 402 182 Fax: +44(0)1415 570 189
email: customerservices@booksource.net

Web orders at www.capercailliebooks.co.uk

Blooded

Isabel Wright

Blooded is a rites of passage play about four sixteen year old girls coming to terms with the loss of childhood and its innocence. The once close bonds between the girls unravel, at times humourously and at times tragically. Wright's vivid portrayal of growing up makes compelling reading.

Blooded comes as a shattering deconstruction of just how fragile this sense of girl power can be . . . there's no denying the intensity of the writing.

The Scotsman

ISBN 0-9549625-4-0

£8.99

Available from Booksource
Tel: +44(0)8702 402 182 Fax: +44(0)1415 570 189
email: customerservices@booksource.net

Web orders at www.capercailliebooks.co.uk

The Life of Stuff

Simon Donald

Sex, drugs and Frank Sinatra: The Life of Stuff is a brilliantly funny fly-on-the-wall snapshot of eight lives careering out of control as small-time crook and aspirant pharmaceutical entrepreneur Willie Dobie's best laid plans unravel when human nature takes its predictably unpredictable course . . . In common with a number of first-rate modern Scottish plays The Life of Stuff has, as yet, only received two professional productions. I fervently hope this new publication will lead to the wider recognition it deserves.

Hugh Hodgart, Head of Acting at RSAMD, Glasgow

Furiously contemporary, extremely funny and has a cast of outrageous yet sympathetic characters which take possession like a cult.

Julie Morrice, Scotland on Sunday

ISBN 0-9545206-6-1

£5.99

Available from Booksource
Tel: +44(0)8702 402 182   Fax: +44(0)1415 570 189
email: customerservices@booksource.net

Web orders at www.capercailliebooks.co.uk

The Waltzer

Rhiannon Tise

The Waltzer is a touching and sensitive exploration of the serious business of growing up. A world of beleaguered single parents and adolescent fears and friendships is reflected in the dark mirror of Sally's experience on her first real date. The garish glamour and hectic motion of the fairground and the Waltzer itself provide a perfect setting for this multi-faceted depiction of the thrills and spills of a teenager's first steps towards the adult world. Written for radio, The Waltzer draws much of its power and point from the complex interaction between past and present events, inner monologue and intercut dialogue. In our film and TV dominated culture we can easily miss out on the imaginative strength of radio drama - the publication of this play is a timely reminder of the real alternatives to the siren call of MTV, Cartoon Network and the Disney Channel.

Hugh Hodgart, Head of Acting at RSAMD, Glasgow

ISBN 0-9545206-3-7

£5.99

Available from Booksource
Tel: +44(0)8702 402 182 Fax: +44(0)1415 570 189
email: customerservices@booksource.net

Web orders at www.capercailliebooks.co.uk

King Matt

Stephen Greenhorn

King Matt, the story of a boy who becomes a king, is a simple fable filled with surprisingly complex resonances. In common with the very best in storytelling for children, it confronts the big moral issues surrounding the way in which one makes one's way in the world and through life: self-interest vying with self-sacrifice, the greed of the individual with the needs of the collective. The boy-king Matt is undoubtedly the hero of the tale but it is his human faults and frailties as well as his intrepid spirit that keep us on the edge of our seats right up to the suspense-filled ending. This is a play written for children that children would have great fun playing for themselves.

Hugh Hodgart, Head of Acting at RSAMD, Glasgow

A highly articulate play that speaks volumes about the nature of democracy and personal responisibility.

The Stage

ISBN 0-9545206-2-9

£5.99

Available from Booksource
Tel: +44(0)8702 402 182   Fax: +44(0)1415 570 189
email: customerservices@booksource.net

Web orders at www.capercailliebooks.co.uk

Dr Korczak's Example

David Greig

Dr Korczak's Example is set in the final, numbered, days of an orphanage in the Warsaw ghetto in 1942. Based on real events, this 'Brechtian' retelling generates an almost unbearable power and pathos through the simple humanity, warts and all, of the central characters who are trapped both by the inexorable forces of Nazi oppression and by our fore-knowledge of the fate that awaits them. The play's 'alienation' device of depicting its characters through the use of dolls, further enhances our painful feeling of powerlessness. Yet, in spite of its tragic outcome, Dr Korczak's Example, like the real life of its protagonist, leaves us exhilarated and uplifted by the indomitable power of love.

Hugh Hodgart, Head of Acting at RSAMD, Glasgow

This is the dramatist's art turned to serve an idea of theatre which is unreproducable in any other medium – a play not to forget.

Will Hutton, The Observer

ISBN 0-9545206-1-0

£5.99

Available from Booksource

Tel: +44(0)8702 402 182 Fax: +44(0)1415 570 189

email: customerservices@booksource.net

Web orders at www.capercailliebooks.co.uk